The Soul Bird

To my beloved children Tal, Laliv and Tamar

The Soul Bird

Michal Snunit

Illustrated by
Na'ama Golomb

ROBINSON
London

Deep down, inside our bodies,
lives the soul.

No one has ever seen it,
but we all know it's there.

Not only do we know it's there,
we know what's in it, too.

Inside the soul,
right in the very middle of it,
there's a bird standing on one foot.

This is the soul bird.

It feels everything we feel.

When someone hurts our feelings,
the soul bird runs round and round in pain.

When someone loves us,
it hops and skips
up and down
backwards and forwards.

When someone calls our name,
it listens carefully
to hear what kind of call it is.

When someone is angry with us,
it curls itself into a ball
and is silent and sad.

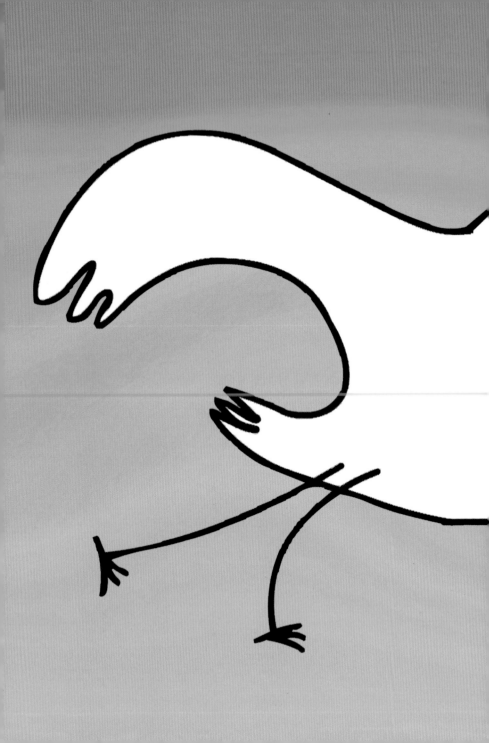

And when someone hugs us,
the soul bird, deep down inside,
grows and grows until it almost fills us.

That's how good it feels
when someone hugs us.

Deep down, inside, lives the soul.

No one has ever seen it,
but we all know it's there.

Never, never has a person been born
who didn't have a soul.

It sparks the moment we are born
and never leaves us –
not even once –
for as long as we live.

It's like the air that people breathe
from the moment they are born
until the time they die.

Do you want to know
what the soul bird is made of?

Well, it's really quite simple:
it's made of drawers.

These drawers can't be opened
just like that –
because each is locked
with its own special key!

Only the soul bird can open these drawers.

How?

Ah, that's quite simple too:
with its other foot.

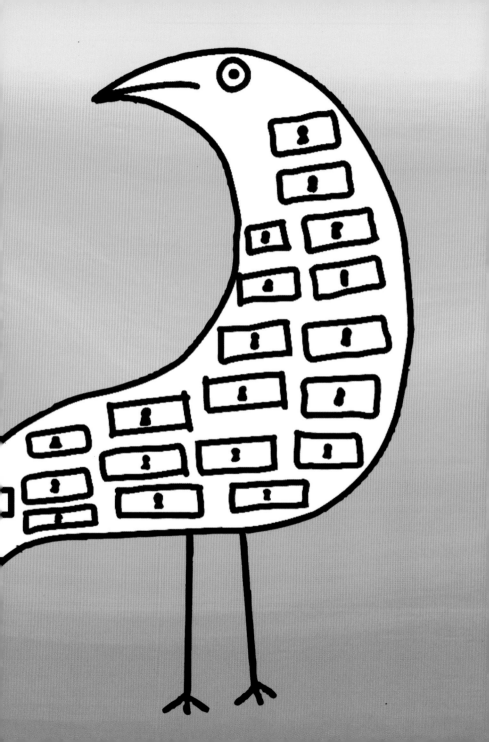

The soul bird stands on one foot,
and with its other foot
(tucked under its wing when it's resting)
it turns the key to the drawer it
wants to open, pulls the handle,
and lets everything inside – out!

Because there is a drawer
for everything we feel,
the soul bird has many, many drawers:
one for being happy and one for being sad;
one for being jealous and one for being content;
one for being hopeful and one for being hopeless;
one for being patient and one for being impatient.

There is also one for hating
and one for being loved.

There is even a drawer for being lazy
and one for being vain.

And there is a special drawer for your deepest
secrets – which is hardly ever opened.

There are other drawers too – whatever
drawers you dream of.

Sometimes you can tell the bird
which key to turn and which drawers to open.

Sometimes the bird will choose
especially for you.

Like, when you want to be silent and order
the soul bird to open the silence drawer.

But the bird decides all by itself
to open the talking drawer
and you talk and talk without even wanting to.

You want to listen patiently, but the soul bird
opens his impatience drawer
and you become impatient.

Sometimes you get jealous
without meaning to.

And sometimes you get in the way
when you only want to help.

The soul bird does not always do what it
is told and gets things in a mess.

By now you've understood that everyone is different because there's a different soul bird deep inside.

The bird which opens the happiness drawer each day pours happiness into your body and you will be happy.

But if the bird opens the anger drawer
he will be angry until the bird
closes the drawer behind him.

A bird who feels bad will open up
the drawers which make you feel bad.

A bird who feels good will open up
the drawers which make you feel good.

Most important is to listen to the soul bird,
because sometimes it calls us
and we don't hear it.

This is a shame – it wants to tell us
about ourselves.

It wants to tell us about the feelings
that are locked up inside its drawers.

Some of us hear it all the time.
Some almost never.

And some of us hear it
only once in a lifetime.

That's why it's a good idea –
maybe late at night
when everything is quiet –
to listen to the soul bird
deep down inside us.

ROBINSON

First published in Great Britain in 1998 by Robinson Publishing
This revised and updated edition published in 2010 by Robinson

Text copyright © EL-AZ Ltd and Michal Snunit, 1998, 2010
Illustrations copyright © Na'ama Golomb 1998, 2010
Background paintings © Diane Law, 2010

3 5 7 9 10 8 6 4

The moral right of the author has been asserted.

A CIP catalogue record for this book
is available from the British Library.

ISBN: 978-1-84901-032-0

Printed and bound in Malaysia by Tien Wah Press

Robinson
An imprint of
Little, Brown Book Group
Carmelite House
50 Victoria Embankment
London EC4Y 0DZ

An Hachette UK Company
www.hachette.co.uk

www.improvementzone.co.uk